This poignant photograph at the former Mittersill Ski Area was taken in 1982, just after the ski area closed. Despite fairly high annual snowfall and snowmaking, Mittersill Ski Area succumbed to competition and financial pressures. During the last two decades, some trails were kept clear by backcountry skiers, and as of early 2008, plans were being developed to reopen the ski area as a part of next-door Cannon Mountain. *Courtesy Dorothy I. Crossley.*

LOST SKI AREAS

of the

White Mountains

Roger M. Clemons
P. O. Box 102
Bartlett, NH 03812

JEREMY K. DAVIS

Foreword by Glenn Parkinson of the New England Ski Museum

Charleston H London

THE
History
PRESS

Published by The History Press
Charleston, SC 29403
www.historypress.net

Cover images courtesy of the New England Ski Museum, Dick Smith and Sandra Schmiedeknecht.
All images are courtesy of the author unless otherwise stated.

First published 2008
Second printing 2009
Third printing 2009

Manufactured in the United States

ISBN 978.1.59629.479.0

Davis, Jeremy K.
Lost ski areas of the White Mountains / Jeremy K. Davis.
p. cm.
ISBN 978-1-59629-479-0
1. Skis and skiing--White Mountains (N.H. and Me.)--Guidebooks. 2. White Mountains (N.H. and Me.)--
Guidebooks. I. Title.
GV854.5.W46D38 2008
796.9309742'2--dc22
2008022540

Notice: The information in this book is true and complete to the best of our knowledge. It is offered without guarantee on the part of the author or The History Press. The author and The History Press disclaim all liability in connection with the use of this book.

Contents

Foreword

Skiing's history includes the facts and figures of its past. Details such as winners of races and lists of ski areas that are no longer open are examples of the sport's history. Skiing's heritage goes deeper than that. Heritage encompasses the memories and the feelings of the past. Skiing's heritage is the smell of the wet wool and the taste of the hot chocolate after a day on the snow.

Memories and feelings are personal—we each have our own. Skiing's past is colored by our memories. It is fairly easy to document skiing's history. Because of the personal nature, it is more difficult to document its heritage. When people visit the New England Ski Museum, where Jeremy Davis is on the board of directors, they are always suitably impressed by all the old skis and by the history of the sport. At some point, they come to a pair of skis and stop. With emotion or wonder, they point at the skis and say, "I learned how to ski on a pair of skis just like that." At that point, we have crossed over from history to heritage. It has become personal. We have touched their memories from years back.

People say that they want us to preserve skiing's history, but what they really want is for us to preserve skiing's heritage, to preserve *their* heritage. Many people learned to ski at small, local ski areas in an era when skiing was usually not big business. A local businessman or farmer would put up a lift or rope tow and parents would often staff the lifts and teach skiing. It was a community effort. Many of those areas are now closed, lost to today's skiers.

We may have grown up in different states, but we have shared memories of learning to ski and riding a rope tow, Poma lift or T-bar, and of skiing under the lights on a school night. Jeremy's work reminds us of our youth. By documenting the past of lost ski areas, Jeremy has also documented the sense of community found at a small, local ski hill. He has documented the pride, the work and the fun that was found across the North Country in the winter.

Preserving the history and the heritage of skiing is a noble endeavor. The passing of time brings with it many changes, but they are often more superficial than we may think. Skiing's soul remains unchanged. A sport is richer for having its memories. Jeremy reminds us of the joy we felt as kids riding the rope tows and skiing the boot-packed slopes of our youth.

Glenn Parkinson
New England Ski Museum

Acknowledgements

This book would not be possible without the help of many ski history enthusiasts. Many took time out of their busy schedules to visit lost areas, talk to former owners/operators, dig up old family photos and more.

I must first thank my parents, Ken and Linda Davis, and my brother, Nathan, for their support over the last fifteen years or more. They have come along on many expeditions to lost areas, and have always been there for me.

The staff and board at the New England Ski Museum were a tremendous help. Executive Director Jeff Leich was extremely helpful in acquiring many photos for the book from the museum's archives. Linda Bradshaw was instrumental in finding contacts for several lost ski areas, and Kay Kerr was of great assistance during my research visits. Glenn Parkinson, current board member and former president of the board, is owed a big debt for his initial research on lost ski areas, and for being one of the earliest supporters of New England Lost Ski Areas Project. He graciously wrote the foreword for this book. E. John Allen, also on the board, provided several images used in the book.

Jeremy Clark, Jon Gallup, Neil Brodein, Fred Schaaff, Dan Robertson, Peter Avedisian, David Metsky, Chris Bradford and Art Donahue all deserve thanks for sending contemporary photos of these lost ski areas.

Nanette Greer Novak, Laurie Puliafico, Sandy Nichols Ward, Mike Sweeney, Woodward Bousquet, Clair Brown and Paul Hudson from the Bethlehem Heritage Society, Richard Hollander, the Kancamagus Ski Area, Emily Langford, Rich Stimpson, Sharon Parent, George Putnam, Sandra Schmiedeknecht, Dale Trecarten, Paul Getchell, Ken Williams, Carol Stevens, Johnny Edge, the Cook Memorial Library and Warren Bartlett all contributed vintage imagery that was invaluable.

Bill Currier, who inspected and built ski lifts throughout New Hampshire and New England for many decades, conveyed to me many little-known stories of these lost areas.

Barbara Smith was very generous to allow us to use her late husband Dick Smith's excellent vintage photos throughout the book.

Professional photographer Dorothy I. Crossley was very helpful with the history of Mittersill, and allowed us to use her exceptional photos of that area.

Andrea Fitzgerald from the Lisbon Historical Society, Lucy Wyman from Mount Prospect and Tara Tower from Lincoln-Woodstock Recreation need to be thanked for their assistance in various areas.

Many thanks go to Susan May, who spent many hours scanning historical Thorn Mountain images and researching lost Jackson ski areas that were used or detailed in this book.

Tom Eastman's research on lost ski areas in the North Conway/Jackson region was extremely beneficial. Tom has also been a big supporter of NELSAP over the years, and his articles on the website have given it much publicity.

For everybody who has contributed to or promoted NELSAP over the last ten years—it is because of you that the website has grown to where it is today.

Finally, to Scott Drake: your enthusiastic support and patience while I wrote this book are greatly appreciated! You have my eternal thanks!

My apologies for any omissions of those who have assisted.

Introduction

Skiing has been an integral part of tourism in the White Mountains for over eighty years. Countless skiers have enjoyed the many fine ski areas than have operated in this region. Sadly, due to many factors, sixty ski areas have now become "lost," and are no longer operating.

A lost ski area is defined as having some kind of uphill transportation. Any kind of lift applies, from a rope tow, to a chairlift, to a railroad. While there are numerous abandoned ski trails that were not served by lifts in the White Mountains, they technically do not meet the definition of a lost ski area. As with all things in life, there are a few exceptions to this rule. Peckett's, an open slope that had the first ski school in the United States, is featured, as is the Nansen Ski Jump, a historical jump in Berlin used for nearly fifty years.

The development of ski areas and ski resorts rapidly took off once the first rope tow in New England opened in Woodstock, Vermont, in 1934. The following year, New Hampshire saw its first rope tow open, at the now lost Trevena Farm in Lisbon, New Hampshire. Four years later, fifty ski areas would be in operation!

While some ski areas would cease operation altogether during World War II, many new areas opened shortly afterward. The founders of these ski areas were often young men returning from service in the Tenth Mountain Division during the war. These former soldiers, who had spent time in the Alps, were ready to begin their careers; with the growing popularity of skiing, they were a natural fit to open ski areas.

During the 1950s and 1960s, the number of resorts in the White Mountains exploded. Chairlifts and gondolas sprouted up at the larger resorts, while T-bars and Poma lifts opened up at some of the former rope tow areas. This was skiing's heyday in the White Mountains, when countless skiers came from all over to enjoy the many and growing resorts.

By the 1970s, however, numerous factors began to take their toll on many of the smaller ski areas. A series of gas crises impacted the average family's ability to make long trips to ski areas. Liability insurance rates rose for many of the small ski areas due to an increased number of lawsuits. Volunteerism began to drop at many of the community ski areas. And several poor snow seasons in the late 1970s and early 1980s made some ski areas impossible to open.

One by one, the smaller areas began to close, slowly at first, and then rapidly by the early 1980s. Even a few larger ski areas, such as Mittersill and Tyrol, were not immune, closing in the early 1980s. Finally, by 2008, out of the seventy-one ski areas that once existed in the White Mountains, only thirteen were left.

Will any of these lost areas return? It is known that some ski areas will never return, such as Thorn Mountain, due to the numerous homes now built on the former slopes. Others have completely grown in and would require much work to reopen. A few reopenings are possible, including the rope tow in Lisbon—although operations have been suspended over the last several years, it is still maintained. Also, there are plans by the State of New Hampshire to reopen Mittersill over the coming years, and by the time you read this, it may have reopened.

For this book, the White Mountains Region is roughly defined along a line running from Piermont, to Plymouth, to West Ossipee, to the border with Maine and then northward to the Canadian border. Our tour of the lost ski areas of the White Mountains begins in the Plymouth Region and then goes clockwise through northwest and northern New Hampshire, the Eastern Slopes region and finally ends in West Ossipee.

Lost Ski Areas of the Plymouth Region

Plymouth and the surrounding towns were some of the earliest ski destinations in the state of New Hampshire. Being located on the southern fringe of the White Mountains, Plymouth was closer to population centers farther south, including Boston about 125 miles away. "Snow trains" made frequent visits, allowing skiers from cities to enjoy a weekend of skiing in the region.

The earliest ski area in Plymouth was Frontenac, started in the mid-1930s, but Mount Pero and Huckins Hill opened shortly thereafter. A fourth ski area, Wendy's, opened about 1940, and was located on the same hill as Frontenac. Wendelin Hilty, a Swiss who had founded the first ski school in Chile, led the Plymouth Ski School at Wendy's Slope. The rope tow that operated there (just for ski lessons) is believed to have been the first of its kind in America. Famous ski instructors from Europe, like Hilty, were very important to early ski areas as the sport was so unfamiliar to many New Englanders.

Huckins Hill was also very historic, boasting one of the first overhead cable lifts in New Hampshire. The area was part of Fred Pabst's Ski Tows Inc., an early chain of ski areas. Mount Pero Lodge was also one of the first complete ski resorts with slopeside lodging to operate in New Hampshire.

In time, Frontenac closed, but Wendy's Slope took its name, and Huckins Hill would be closed during World War II. The Holderness School opened a rope tow for students in the 1950s, and another tow opened at the Rumney Bible Conference in the 1960s, but these would be closed by the 1980s. Campton Mountain in the Waterville Estates, a ski area with a chairlift, would close in the early 2000s. The only survivor in the Plymouth Region is Tenney Mountain, which has also closed several times, but appears to be on the right track for survival.

Additional ski areas not pictured include:

Bel'Air Lodge, West Rumney: A 900-foot-long rope tow served a novice slope and several trails here in the late 1930s. Along with skiing, skating, sleighing and snowshoeing, tobogganing was also available.

Gateway Townhomes, Campton: A 550-foot-long rope tow operated near the Gateway Townhomes off of Gateway Road. The exact years of operation are unknown.

1 Huckins' Hill
1800 ft. Cable Ski Tramway—
6 Trails

2 Mt. Pero
Ski Tow—Lodge

3 Frontenac
Ski Tow—Swiss Chalet—
2 Trails—Floodlighted

4 Wendy's Slopes
Home of Swiss Ski School—
Ski Tow—Club House

5 To Cannon Mt.
and Aerial Tramway

Plymouth, New Hampshire, was an early center for skiers, with access via automobile, Friday night snow trains from New York City or daily trains from Boston. Four ski areas were developed from the mid-1930s to the early 1940s: Wendy's Slope and Frontenac on Stage Coach Mountain, Mount Pero Lodge and Huckins Hill. *Courtesy New England Ski Museum.*

Plymouth
NEW HAMPSHIRE

WENDELIN O. HILTY

Swiss Instructor

of

PLYMOUTH

SKI SCHOOL

JOIN THE PARADE - SKI PLYMOUTH FIRST

Wendelin Hilty, a Swiss ski instructor who founded the first ski school in Chile, ran the Swiss Ski School, first at Frontenac Ski Area on the north side of Stage Coach Mountain, and then at his own slope, Wendy's, complete with a rope tow on the east side. *Courtesy E. John Allen.*

Frontenac Ski Area was planned and laid out by the champion ski racer Dick Durrance and by Sel Hannah, soon to be a well-known ski area designer in the late 1930s. As this trail map shows, one wide-open slope was flanked by several narrow trails, including the very steep Durrance Devil Dip Trail. A "colorful" Swiss chalet was located off the Frontenac Trail and served as a warming hut. *Courtesy E. John Allen.*

The popular Frontenac slope, off of Parker Street, is shown here along with the ski shelter middle left. The rope tow is just to the left of this image, and was described in a late 1930s brochure as "servicing the newly cleared open slopes and trails, thus sparing you the tedious up-climbs."

FRONTENAC SKI DEVELOPMENT, PLYMOUTH, NEW HAMPSHIRE
TWO SKI TOWS—TWO OPEN SLOPES—SIX TRAILS

After World War II, Frontenac and Wendy's became one area again, with interconnected trails. This 1940s postcard indicates two lifts, showing that the two areas had merged; it kept the Frontenac name, but occasionally was referred to as the "Plymouth Slopes Area."

This trail map shows the merged areas in the 1940s. The East Slope was the original Wendy's, with the North Slope being the original Frontenac. Note that the Durrance Devil Dip Trail (4) appears again in this trail map. This trail would eventually become the location of a T-bar. The north side would gradually fall out of use, and in 1960, Plymouth rezoned the land as residential, permanently closing that section. The entire ski area remained closed for a few years. *Courtesy Nanette Greer Novak.*

In 1962, George and Nancy Greer purchased the original Wendy's area and called the area "Frontenac Ski Camp," a private ski area with overnight lodging for young skiers. George's brother Alfred and his wife Della were also owners of the camp from 1962 to 1969. Over the next thirty years, countless youngsters would learn how to ski at the area. Pictured here is the interior of the lodge in 1963 with some of the Greer family in Swiss-themed clothing for a promotional photo. *Courtesy Nanette Greer Novak.*

The main slope continued to be served by the original rope tow until 1968, when the steepest T-bar in New England was installed on the former Durrance Devil Dip Trail, just to the right of this 1973 shot of the East Slope. Note the power lines in the middle of the photo that bisected the ski area. *Courtesy Nanette Greer Novak.*

A view looking down the lower East Slope shows the ski lodge and a beginner rope tow. Numerous other trails, named after the children of the two Greer families, snaked their way through the woods, including Betsy's Bump, Hanky Panky, Nan-Del, the Staff-a-nack, the Verge, Cui-Bee, Leaping Lar, Sissy's Swirl and the Blank Wall. *Courtesy Nanette Greer Novak.*

After a fresh snowfall, this snowcat, parked outside the lodge, was used to pack the snow with the attached snow roller. The lodge was the hub of the ski camp, and every camper that has written to NELSAP remembers the Greers as a wonderful and kind family. *Courtesy Nanette Greer Novak.*

In 1991, the area ceased operating as a ski area due to several poor snow seasons. The area was briefly resurrected in 1994–95 by Dan Burgess and renamed Lynx Creek, but this did not succeed. In 2002, the property was put up for sale by George Greer. This visit to Frontenac in May showed the ski lodge to be in good shape. The beginner tow, on the far right, was still partially standing.

The steep T-bar was still standing in 2002 as well. Completely intact as viewed from the summit, the Ts still clung to the cable and were fully retractable. The liftline had begun to grow in, with three- to five-foot-high brush common on the lower section of the liftline. A website dedicated to Frontenac, complete with archive video, can be viewed at http://www.frontenacskicamp.org.

Peter Avedisian purchased and removed the T-bar later in 2002 and installed it at his private ski area, Cosmic Hill, in the Mad River Valley in Vermont. This is the same tower that was still standing in 2002. Although Frontenac Ski Area is now gone, a small piece of it still operates at Cosmic Hill. View video and photos of the refurbished T-bar at http://www.cosmichill.com. *Courtesy Peter Avedisian.*

MT. PERO SKI TOW

900 FOOT TOW

On 45 Acre Open Slope, Vertical Descent 150 feet.

Plenty Space and Variety of Slopes.

IN THIS SAME FIELD IS

MT. PERO LODGE

Designed for the Comfort of Skiers.

Accommodates 52.

Has a 30 x 60 Main Room on lower floor where skiers lounge and eat.

Large Field Stone Fire Place.

Sleeping Quarters on Upper Floor.

Each room contains 2 double deck single bunks.

RATES $5.00 PER DAY

Includes a Comfortable Bed, 3 Square Meals of Farm Food

AND USE OF SKI TOW AND TRAILS

For Reservations, Address:

SAM T. PAGE

PLYMOUTH, N. H.

Above: Mount Pero was sold to Frank and Peg Favorat, who continued operating the area for ski clubs, and even ran a ski camp similar to, but smaller than, Frontenac during the 1970s. This patch belongs to Richard Hollander, who skied at the camp in 1971 during school vacation week. *Courtesy Richard Hollander.*

Left: The Mount Pero Lodge in Campton, originally owned by Sam Page, operated a rope tow from the mid-1930s to the 1970s. In the late 1930s, Mount Pero was rare in that it offered skiing and lodging. Ski clubs and small groups frequented this 150-foot vertical ski area. The lodge was at the top of the slope, making this an upside-down ski area. *Courtesy E. John Allen.*

Richard Hollander remembers that a typical day of camp would consist of ski lessons in the morning, lunch and then more skiing in the afternoon. By the end of the week, racing was introduced, as well as an awards night on the last night. Pictured here is the side of the lodge. *Courtesy Richard Hollander.*

Richard is pictured here outside the lodge in 1971. Mount Pero closed sometime about 1980, but the rope tow still stands as of 2008. The lodge is well maintained as a private home. *Courtesy Richard Hollander.*

Left: Huckins Hill in Plymouth operated from the late 1930s to the early 1940s. Founded by Fred Pabst, Huckins Hill was one of the first ski areas in New England to operate with a J-bar lift. Six slopes and one six-hundred-foot-wide slope were served by the eighteen-hundred-foot-long J-bar. The ski area did not operate after World War II, like most of Pabst's areas, and the lift was removed and reinstalled at Bromley Mountain in Vermont. No trace of this ski area remains today. *Courtesy E. John Allen.*

Below: The Rumney Bible Conference in Rumney operated an approximately 850-foot-long rope tow on a 150-foot vertical drop for guests during the 1970s. This aerial image shows the two slopes that were used for skiing. The slopes are used today for tubing for guests at the camp. *Courtesy NASA World Wind.*

Holderness School in Holderness operated a ski area for students from the 1950s to the 1970s that was constructed by Don Henderson and others. Students would train on these two wide slopes, which were served by a rope tow. Also note the much larger Tenney Mountain still open in the background. Eventually, the ski program migrated to larger mountains—Cannon for the alpine skiers, and Waterville Valley for freestyle. *Courtesy NASA World Wind.*

Campton Mountain in Campton operated from 1969 to 2003 in the Waterville Estates. Originally called Locke Waterville, a double chair and rope tow served these slopes on a three-hundred-foot vertical drop. The area operated sporadically in the late 1990s and early 2000s due to some poor snow years, and in 2003, the decision was made to close the ski area. *Courtesy NASA World Wind.*

In 2007, the base lodge and loading area for the double chairlift are shown empty of the skiers who once enjoyed Campton Mountain. To the right, not pictured, was the beginner rope tow slope. *Courtesy Jeremy Clark.*

While the double chairlift still stands and appears functional, the main ski slope has begun to grow in, beginning the process that most lost ski areas embark upon after closing. *Courtesy Jeremy Clark.*

Lost Ski Areas
of the Northwestern
White Mountains

The Northwestern White Mountains Region was home to many lost ski areas. From the first rope tow in New Hampshire (Trevena Hill) to the largest ski area to close (Mittersill), this region is chock full of history.

While several trails were built in this region, widespread skiing did not truly develop until Peckett's opened a ski school on Sugar Hill during the 1929–30 season. Organized ski instruction, under the tutelage of Sig Buchmayr, allowed pupils to progress rapidly. In 1935, the first rope tow opened at Trevena Hill in Lisbon, and within a few years rope tows were popping up everywhere.

Competition from much larger ski areas is high in this region. The success of Cannon, Waterville Valley and Loon gave ski areas a much larger alternative than the smaller rope tows. All but one of the small rope tow ski areas that once operated here are gone. Even having a chairlift was no guarantee of success—both Mittersill and Monteau had double chairs but closed. There is, however, a chance that Mittersill may reopen, as the state has developed plans to connect it with Cannon Mountain Ski Area.

One ski area in this region that does not quite meet the definition of being lost is Snow's Mountain at Waterville Valley. While alpine skiing no longer takes place, the double chairlift is occasionally used for cross-country ski races, and a cross-country trail that requires a lift ticket does run down an old ski slope. The lift has also been used recently for mountain biking in the summer.

Additional lost ski areas not pictured include:

Henry Slope, Lincoln: This ski area briefly operated in the late 1930s on Pollard Road. Today, the area has been developed for housing.

Tamarack Slope, Franconia: In the mid- to late 1940s, a rope tow one thousand feet in length operated on the lower slopes of Kinsman Mountain.

Trevena Hill, Lisbon: The first rope tow in New Hampshire opened on January 20, 1935, across from the Trevena Farm. According to Andrea Fitzgerald, Harlan Jesseman constructed the tow, and John Bailey of Lisbon was the first to ride the rope tow. The rope for the tow had come from the tow in Woodstock, Vermont. That tow was lengthened, and the old rope was then used at Trevena.

Cheney Farm, Lisbon: The rope tow from Trevena was moved to the Cheney Farm off of Pearl Lake Road, where it operated in the 1940s and 1950s.

Dickinson Slope, Lisbon: A one-thousand-foot-long rope tow operated in the late 1930s at the Dickinson Farm.

Gardner Mountain, Woodsville: The Silver Fox Outing Club operated a 1,000-foot-long rope tow on a 360-foot-drop from the late 1930s to the mid-1950s at Gardner Mountain.

Oscar Bedor's Farm Tow, Monroe: The Monroe Men's Club staffed a rope tow in the 1950s and early 1960s at Oscar Bedor's farm. Hot cocoa was served at a small shelter at the bottom. A wide-open slope was available for skiers.

Joy Farm Hill, Bath: According to Mary Ruppert, the Joy Farm Hill once operated a rope tow on a wide slope. While the ski area is now closed, towers for the rope tow still stand.

KINSMAN PEMIGEWASSET CANNON PROFILE EAGLE CLIFF LAFAYETTE LINCOLN HAYSTACK LIBERTY MT. FLUME COOLIDGES WHALEBACK POTASH KNOB

FRANCONIA NOTCH ROAD

TO TRAMWAY
U.S. ROUTE 3

SLOPE

SKATING RINK

NORTH WOODSTOCK

LOST RIVER ROAD

PARKING AREA

SLOPE

Grandview Mountain
SKI TOW AND SLOPE
1000 FOOT TOW
1200 FOOT SLOPE
240 FT. ELEVATION
Suitable for all Grades of Skiers

Bromley · Boston

Grandview Mountain in North Woodstock offered a wide-open slope and one-thousand-foot-long rope tow during the 1950s. Al Huot was the operator of Grandview. The name was no accident—there was a "grand view" to the north, looking toward Franconia Notch. The slope at Grandview was named "Surprise," and was about one-fifth of a mile long. Also note that another slope (not served by a lift) was located just north of Lost River Road.

COME TO *North Woodstock*
NEW HAMPSHIRE

Excellent TOW·SLOPES·TRAILS

Close to Cannon Mt. Aerial Tramway

This 1950s brochure advertised the tow and slopes, but also the nearby Cannon Mountain aerial tramway. While skiers would stop in North Woodstock to ski at Grandview, many locals would walk to the ski area due to its proximity to town.

Al Huot stands at the top of the slope in the 1950s, looking north in the general direction of Franconia Notch. Today, the area is private property and grown in. The Grandview Estates were built up around the former ski area. The rope tow eventually made its way to King Grants Inn, now another lost ski area near Laconia. *Courtesy Al Huot and Kancamagus Ski Area.*

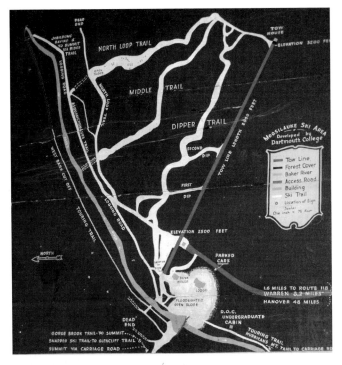

Left: Moosilauke Ski Area was located at the Moosilauke Ravine Lodge in Woodstock, and was developed by the Dartmouth Outing Club. According to David Metsky, the trails were originally cut prior to World War II, but were not used until the late 1940s. The trails were recut in 1947 or 1948, when a two-thousand-foot-long rope tow was installed. In 1951 and 1952, the Dartmouth Winter Carnival was held here due to a lack of snow in Hanover. *Courtesy David Metsky.*

Below: The ski area closed about 1953 due to difficult winter access and competition from other nearby ski areas. By 2004, the ski area had completely grown in, with the ski trails now invisible. However, the liftline is still faintly visible through these birch trees. *Courtesy David Metsky.*

Above left: Swiftwater Valley in Woodsville, New Hampshire, was one of the last new ski areas to open in New England. Opened in December of 1973 in the Mountain Lakes development, the area was quickly renamed Monteau. While Monteau catered mostly to homeowners, it was open to the public and offered uncrowded skiing.

Above right: These three images come from a mid-1970s brochure, and show the 2,800-foot-long chairlift, chairlift unload and a ski chalet.

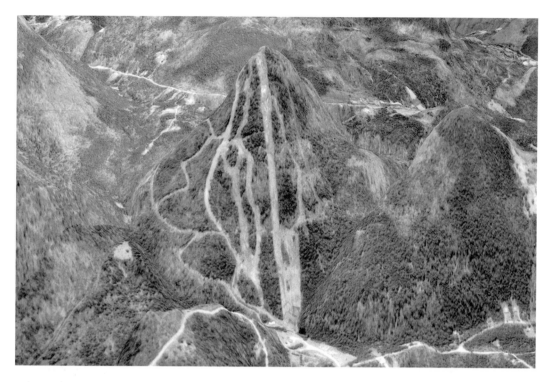

This aerial view of the ski area from 1993 shows the ten trails and slopes that Monteau offered. Note the mix of wider slopes and narrower trails. Ten miles of Nordic skiing were also available. Snow making was installed on some trails in 1983. *Courtesy NASA World Wind.*

In 1989, the mountain was leased out, and the area declared bankruptcy in the spring of 1990. In 1992, Nashoba Valley, a popular Massachusetts ski area, purchased the chairlift, hired a helicopter and removed the lift just after Labor Day. An early morning shot on the day of the removal shows the lift on its final day at Monteau. *Courtesy David McPhee.*

Within a short period of time, as helicopter rates were very expensive, the helicopter plucked the last remaining chairlift tower and airlifted it to a waiting flatbed truck in the parking lot. This lift would soon be refurbished and reopened as the Sundance Triple at Nashoba Valley in December 1994. *Courtesy David McPhee.*

The base lodge in 2008, while not being used anymore for skiing, is still standing and used for functions during the summer. Mountain Lakes (http://www.mtlakesnh.com) continues to be an active four-season recreational community with two lakes, hiking trails and plenty of outdoor activities. *Courtesy Jon Gallup.*

Much of the mountain has grown in significantly as of the winter of 2008. The chairlift line in the center of the photo has shown rapid tree growth over the past several years. Another slope to the right, which was once served by the rope tow, has been kept fairly clear, and is used by Mountain Lakes for sledding and for Winterfest activities. *Courtesy Jon Gallup.*

The Forest Acres Hotel in Franconia operated a rope tow for guests during the 1940s and 1950s. The hotel became the location of Franconia College in 1963, and students would occasionally fire up the rope tow for some skiing. The area gradually fell into disuse and has grown in today. This aerial view shows the two wide slopes of the ski area, along with Interstate 93. *Courtesy NASA World Wind.*

Baron Hubert von Pantz founded the Mittersill Club Ski Area in 1945 on the north slope of Cannon Mountain. Having owned the Mittersill Club in Tirol, Austria, in the 1930s, the baron left once the Nazis invaded in 1938; seven years later, he opened a new Mittersill Club in Franconia, which had a distinct Alpine theme. *Courtesy New England Ski Museum.*

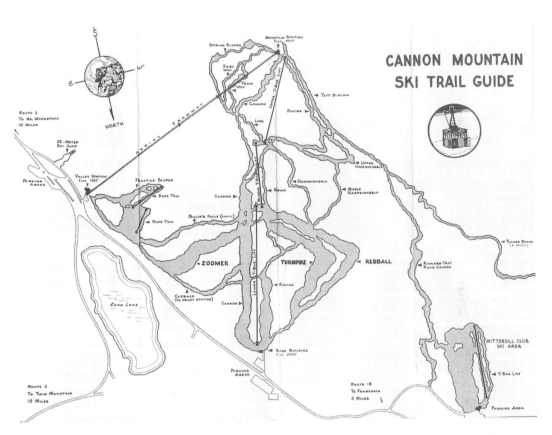

Mittersill Ski Area has always been connected to nearby Cannon Mountain. The lower portions of the Richard Taft Racecourse ended very close to Mittersill. In this 1950s trail map, Mittersill (lower right) had a 1,500-foot-long T-bar that served a wide-open slope and a narrower trail on a 350-foot vertical drop. *Courtesy New England Ski Museum.*

Baron Hubert von Pantz and his wife Terry are shown here in the later years of Mittersill, in 1981, with a view of the ski area in the background. The baron developed an inn at Mittersill along with many private chalet lots, which helped finance the development of Mittersill. *Courtesy Dorothy I. Crossley.*

This 1960s view from the inn shows the expansive wide-open slopes that the baron constructed to simulate skiing in Austria. A 2,500-foot-long T-bar was installed parallel to the earlier T-bar about 1960 and can be seen at the right. The wide slope on the left is the original Taft Slope.

This 1950s view shows the original Taft Slope, with the Taft Racecourse feeding into the slope at the top. To access the Taft Racecourse, skiers would need to ski the Taft Slalom at Cannon, hike up a ridge and then ski back down the Mittersill side.

Air View
Franconia Notch
New Hampshire

This 1960s postcard shows Mittersill on the lower right and Cannon Mountain just above it. Note Mittersill's wide-open slopes and numerous chalets; it was the first ski community built at any New England ski area.

In the 1950s, Mittersill became one of the first ski areas in New England to install snowmaking. This early 1960s view shows an early snow gun from Larchmont Engineering in operation. *Courtesy Dorothy I. Crossley.*

Above: Deep snowfall covers the lower Taft Slope in the 1960s. According to Dorothy Crossley, the original inn was torn down in 1967, and a much larger inn was opened on the same location in the summer of 1968. The inn is visible at the bottom of the slope. *Courtesy Dick Smith.*

Right: The baron was quite the socialite and often had famous visitors to the resort. Lucille Ball and Gary Morton visited the area in 1963, along with her children Lucie Arnaz and Desi Arnaz Jr. According to Dorothy Crossley, Lucille Ball was not allowed to risk injury by skiing, though, due to her insurance policy. *Courtesy Dorothy I. Crossley.*

A lift operator grabs a T-bar and passes it to a girl waiting to ride the lift. This was the original T-bar. The newer (circa 1960) T-bar is on the left. *Courtesy Dorothy I. Crossley.*

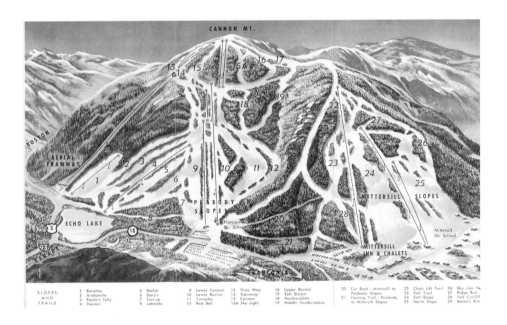

In 1966, a Hall double chairlift with a vertical drop of nearly 1,300 feet was installed, increasing the vertical drop by 500 feet. This trail map shows Mittersill at that time. The area was sporadically marketed with Cannon Mountain, which is why both ski areas were shown on this map. The baron now had a run named after him, Baron's Run, seen at the top of the chairlift. *Courtesy New England Ski Museum.*

A skier races underneath the chairlift in the late 1970s on a powder day. Note the full parking lot on the right, and the inn and numerous chalets in the middle and on the left. In the late 1970s, new management under the Franconia Development Company began to transform the inn to time shares, and the focus was taken off the ski area. *Courtesy Dorothy I. Crossley.*

Sadly, the ski area closed in 1982 due to increased regulation regarding the further development of ski areas and a new focus on the timeshares. Cannon Mountain was now marketed as the ski area of choice for time share owners. Since the ski area was on National Forest land, skiers continued to use the ski area by hiking up and skiing down, and some trails continued to be cleared by skiers. This March 2008 view shows that many of the trails are still recognizable from a distance.

A closer view of the lower slopes in March of 2008 shows the longer T-bar (center) still standing and all of the lower slopes clear. The original T-bar, just to the right of the longer one, still has some towers standing and one can still make out the liftline.

The double chairlift is still standing, sans chairs, in February of 2008. Cannon Mountain has also begun to use the parking lot next to this chairlift as overflow parking. *Courtesy Jeremy Clark.*

Looking up the chairlift line, one notices that the higher elevation towers are about ready to disappear under rapid tree growth. *Courtesy Jeremy Clark.*

Higher up, some skiers have cleared away the growth, and the chairlift becomes much more visible. Some chalets can be clearly seen in the middle of the photograph. *Courtesy Jeremy Clark.*

The unloading ramp at the summit of the ski area almost looks functional, but it has actually deteriorated quite a bit under all the snow. The connector trail from Cannon would be just to the left of this photograph. *Courtesy Jeremy Clark.*

A view midway up the longer T-bar shows the towers still standing, with the liftline quite clear. Some skiers descend from the summit down this liftline. *Courtesy Jeremy Clark.*

Above: The top of the long T-bar still stands, along with the operator's hut. While old electrical wiring remains on the tower, the cables that held the Ts are no longer attached here. *Courtesy Jeremy Clark.*

Right: Peckett's on Sugar Hill, while never offering lift-served skiing, played a crucial role in the development of skiing in New England. America's first ski school opened at Peckett's during the 1929–30 season. Sig Buchmayr, an accomplished Austrian skier, taught lessons there during the 1930s. Later, he would own and operate several ski shops. *Courtesy New England Ski Museum.*

Skiing at Peckett's was strictly a hike-up-and-ski-down affair, with spectacular views of the Northern White Mountains. In the mid-1930s, before nearby Cannon Mountain became lift served, Buchmayr would bring more advanced students to the Taft Trail at Cannon. The growth of Cannon in the late 1930s and early 1940s ended ski instruction at Peckett's. *Courtesy Laurie Puliafico.*

The first rope tow in New Hampshire opened in Lisbon on Trevena Hill on January 20, 1935. Run by the Lisbon Outing Club, skiing was eventually moved closer to town off of Grafton Street in 1959. According to Andrea Fitzgerald from the Lisbon Historical Society, the tow was purchased from Mittersill. Two slopes with a 110-foot vertical drop were bifurcated by a 500-foot-long rope tow. This 2008 view shows the slopes to be quite clear. *Courtesy Jon Gallup.*

All the equipment for the rope tow remains as of 2008, and while the operations have been suspended over the last several years, the area is not officially closed. Skiers would board the lift here. Loose clothing, scarves or long hair were prohibited due to the possibility of them becoming entangled in the rope. There is a chance that the Lions Club may reactivate this ski area. *Courtesy Jon Gallup.*

A very small ski area operated in Remich Park from the 1940s to the 1960s. The rope tow was only 265 feet long! Bill Scheib used to ski there in the mid-1950s, and remembers that "after school we would go to the park and ski our hearts out until our parents would come and drag us home for supper." Today, the slope is used for sledding purposes. *Courtesy Jon Gallup.*

Mount Eustis, also in Littleton, operated from 1939 until the early 1980s. This view shows the 1,600-foot-long rope tow in its early years—one of the longest in the state at that time. Note the tree being pulled as an early grooming device to break up the snow! Skiers also enjoyed a wide-open slope and a narrower Buddy Nute ski trail. *Courtesy New England Ski Museum.*

According to Bill Nichols, Mount Eustis was originally owned by Wilson Lewis, who sold the ski area in 1947 to George Pepperell. Lights were installed for nighttime skiing, held every Wednesday night. Pepperell also started a ski patrol, for which Bill Nichols, Bob Labonte, Charly Brooks and Charles Kennison volunteered in the early 1950s. This sign, which is now on display at the New England Ski Museum, beckoned skiers to the slopes.

Above: In the mid-1950s, Interstate 93 was built, and truncated the ski area by about one third. This resulted in Mount Eustis closing for a few years. In the late 1950s, however, the town of Littleton restarted skiing at Mount Eustis. This more recent aerial view shows Interstate 93 at the base of the wide slope of the mountain. Skiing continued until the early 1980s. Fundraisers were held to try to raise money for a T-bar, but were unsuccessful, and skiing ended at Mount Eustis. *Courtesy NASA World Wind.*

Right: In early 2008, Mount Eustis is still very clear, and is now adorned with something that early skiers would never have imagined—a cell phone tower! The rope tow towers still stand on the left side of the slope. According to Bill Nichols, the Buddy Nute Ski Trail (not pictured here) has grown in and the lower section has been developed with houses. *Courtesy Neil Brodien.*

The wide-open slope with fresh powder today is enough to beckon snowboarders and skiers who wish to hike up. Plans have recently been introduced to use the area as a town skate park, but it is unlikely that organized skiing will ever return to Mount Eustis. *Courtesy Jon Gallup.*

Lost Ski Areas of the Northern White Mountains

This region of New Hampshire tended to be a bit more isolated from the rest of the state. Snow trains rarely made it this far north, and skiers had to pass quite a few other larger ski areas to reach the Northern Whites. Most ski areas in this region were small, local places, where families skied together.

Despite being farther away from population centers, this area had several notable skiing features. The Nansen Ski Jump was the highest jump east of the Mississippi and hosted an Olympic trial. The Cog Railway opened the newest ski area in New Hampshire in 2004, which lasted a few seasons. During this time, the venerable Cog Railway instantly became the oldest ski lift in the country!

Most rope tow areas had closed by the 1970s, and only one still operates today—Mount Prospect.

Additional lost ski areas not pictured include:

Cate's Hill, Berlin: This ski area operated from the late 1930s until the early 1950s. Located on Cate's Hill, the tow was quite long at 2,500 feet!

Mount Jasper Tow, Berlin: A ski area briefly operated between Mount Jasper and the high school during the late 1940s and into the early 1950s. The tow was vandalized in the early 1950s and never reopened.

Pine Mountain Open Slope, Gorham: A 1,000-foot-long rope was available at Pine Mountain in the late 1930s. Its steep slopes were floodlit for nighttime skiing.

Kimball Hill, Whitefield: Operating in the late 1930s and early 1940s, Kimball hill sported an 800-foot-long rope tow with two trails—Trail No. One and Trail No. Two.

Twin Mountain Slopes, Twin Mountain: A 350-foot-long rope tow operated in Twin Mountain in the late 1930s.

Colebrook Tow: A rope tow operated in the early 1950s on land now occupied by the hospital.

Mount Agassiz in Bethlehem was named after Louis Agassiz, a Swiss-American geologist who was the first to propose that the earth had experienced an ice age. It is certainly appropriate then that a ski area would be developed on this mountain. Several guidebooks listed a 1,700-foot-long rope tow on Mount Agassiz in the mid- to late 1940s, run by the Bethlehem Outing Club. This fell out of use in the 1950s. During the 1962–63 ski season, the Bethlehem Ski Club activated a new ski area on Mount Agassiz. The slope was featured prominently in this brochure during the 1960s. *Courtesy Bethlehem Heritage Society.*

This aerial view in 1993 shows the area has changed little in appearance since the 1960s. Mount Agassiz was a very typical rope tow area for a small town—a wide-open slope and no snow making, but very affordable and fun for those who skied there. *Courtesy NASA World Wind.*

This view of the main slope has a sign that forbids the use of tow grippers. Tow grippers made riding a rope tow easier, as they allowed skiers to wear a belt that had a rope with a clamp attached to it. The clamp would be placed around the moving rope tow and would allow the skier to save his gloves, which often got worn out riding lifts. Tow grippers were dangerous to use, though, if the clamp froze to the rope, and their usage was banned at many small ski areas in the White Mountains. *Courtesy Bethlehem Heritage Society.*

The rope tow is viewed here on the right-hand side of the slope. The tow originally operated at Cannon Mountain, but was moved to Mount Agassiz when the ski area opened. Many learned to ski at Mount Agassiz. According to Carol Boucher and the Bethlehem Heritage Society, 109 skiers took advantage of lessons the first year of operations. *Courtesy Bethlehem Heritage Society.*

Here, a young skier completes a race and obstacle course during the Varney Memorial Race in 1979. The Varney Race was held in memory of Allen Varney, who had donated some of the land for the ski area. According to Claire Brown from the Bethlehem Heritage Society, the area closed during the early 1980s due to competition from much larger resorts nearby, high liability insurance expenses and a lack of volunteers. *Courtesy Bethlehem Heritage Society.*

The Mount Washington Cog Railway operated winter ski trains from 2004 to 2006. When the Cog opened for skiing, it instantly had the oldest "ski lift" in North America—the Cog dates back to 1869! Skiers would board the coal-fired trains at the base and then ride up 1,100 vertical feet to the Waumbek Tank at 3,800 feet in elevation, though novices could ask to be dropped off halfway. Only one trail was used, divided into two sections called Upper and Lower Engineer.

The trail was groomed and even had snow making. Small, gladed sections were also built along the trail. Here, the author enjoys some of the deep snow in the glades. While the Cog no longer offers lift-served skiing as of 2008, snow trains still continue, and the trip is recommended for its spectacular scenery. More information on these trains can be viewed at http://www.thecog.com. *Courtesy Nathan Davis.*

Right: The Nansen Ski Jump in Berlin, while never a lift-served ski area, is a very important piece of "lost" history in New Hampshire. This 170-foot-high jump was constructed in 1936 and was the location of Olympic trials in 1938. The jump was the highest east of the Mississippi River. Many competitions were held here until the early 1980s, when the jump was closed for good. It still stands today, but is rapidly falling apart. *Courtesy Dick Smith.*

Below: The Twelfth Street Tow, located on Twelfth Street in Berlin, New Hampshire, opened in the 1960s; it was owned and operated by the City of Berlin. An 800-foot-long rope tow served a 170-foot vertical drop on a wide slope. According to Robbie Munce, a twenty-meter ski jump was also used by Berlin High School and the Notre Dame High School. The jump had a nickname of "Little Nansen," as jumpers would practice here before the much larger jump in town. The ski area closed in the mid-1970s, was briefly reactivated near 1980 and was closed again by 1981, due to high insurance costs. In 1994, the Berlin Ski Team cleared a swatch of trees so they could practice instead of going to Wildcat, but the slope quickly grew in, as this 1998 photo shows. *Courtesy Dave Hilton.*

In 2008, the Twelfth Street Tow slope had almost completely grown in. Compare this with the view ten years ago—the process of forest succession in New England is quick. The base lodge, which used to serve hot cocoa and snacks, still belongs to the City of Berlin, according to Robbie Munce. *Courtesy Jon Gallup.*

The Gorham Outing Club Slope in Shelburne was originally operated by the Gorham Ski Club in the 1940s. The ski area was essentially one main slope, with a rope tow first on the right side of the slope and then moved to the left side in the early 1960s. Page Dinsmore remembers that during the 1960s, the ski area was jammed on weekends with organized ski lessons from the Outing Club. Linda Kovalik used to ski here, and recalls, "I'll never forget how, as kids, we would run the whole show…collecting tickets, making hot chocolate and actually running the always defunct engines trying to keep the tow operating! Liability would never allow operations to run in the same manner today!" *Courtesy E. John Allen.*

Unfortunately, the ski area closed in the early 1970s. Located next to the Town and Country Motor Lodge off Route 2, the ski area is still fairly clear. This March 2008 view shows the wide-open slope. A snowmobile trail now passes through the former ski area, as do power lines.

Lost Ski Areas of the Eastern Slopes Region

This region was home to the greatest concentration of both open and lost ski areas in the state of New Hampshire. In fact, in just one town, Jackson, at least nine ski areas were available at one point! Excellent access to snow train routes and a direct major road to Boston and Portland allowed skiers easy access to the region.

Many lodges and inns had their own rope tows, with skiers taking advantage of near-private skiing at an affordable rate. Cranmore, still very much open, was the king of skiing in this region, and many smaller ski areas had to compete with both its well-organized ski school and its Skimobile lift.

The largest ski area to close first in New Hampshire (and in all reality east of the Mississippi) was Thorn Mountain in Jackson. Even though it had two single chairlifts, several rope tows and over a dozen slopes, financial difficulties and poor snow led to its demise in the late 1950s.

The majority of the rope tow ski areas had closed by the 1970s, as did some of the smaller cable lift areas like Spruce Mountain and Intervale. By 2008, there were no small ski areas operating in this region, but several, including Black Mountain and Cranmore, still feature a skiing atmosphere similar to when they were founded.

Additional lost ski areas not pictured include:

Ballentine's Pasture, Jackson: A "sleigh tow" operated on Ballentine's Pasture off Carter Notch Road during the late 1930s to the early 1940s.

Guptill Pastures, Jackson: Another brief ski area, a one-thousand-foot tow operated here in the early 1940s.

Thorn Mountain Slopes, Jackson: Dick May relayed this story about a rope tow to Tom Eastman in 2002: A very early rope tow was set up at the lower slopes of Thorn Mountain by Carroll Reed for his ski school in 1936–37. A lack of snow did not permit the tow to operate, and it was subsequently moved to Cranmore the following year. This area had nothing to do with the future Thorn Mountain Ski Area.

May Brothers Tow: The same rope tow that operated at Thorn Mountain and Cranmore made its way to the Stanton Slopes and was later sold to a group of World War II veterans, including Dick and Jack May, who moved the tow to Black Mountain in 1946. The rope tow operated until 1948, when Stan Whitney purchased the land, ending the ski area. The slope is now a part of the Black Mountain Ski Area.

Oak Lee Ski Lodge, Jackson: The Oak Lee Lodge offered up a three-hundred-foot rope tow behind the lodge in the mid- to late 1940s. It was quite the place—advertising a "house-party atmosphere." Today, it is the Shannon Door Pub, located at the junction of Routes 16 and 16A.

White Mountain Inn, Jackson: Yet another lost Jackson ski area, the White Mountain Inn offered skiing for guests in the late 1940s.

North Conway Ski Slope, North Conway: Located off of West Side Road, this small ski area offered nighttime skiing and ten acres of skiing on a 20 percent grade. Ski lessons from Mount Cranmore were occasionally offered here.

Little Moat Slopes, North Conway: A rope tow briefly operated at this ski area at the base of Moat Mountain in the mid-1930s. Richard Kimball, who skied here as a child, remembers that the slope was still visible until about 1950, before disappearing into the forest.

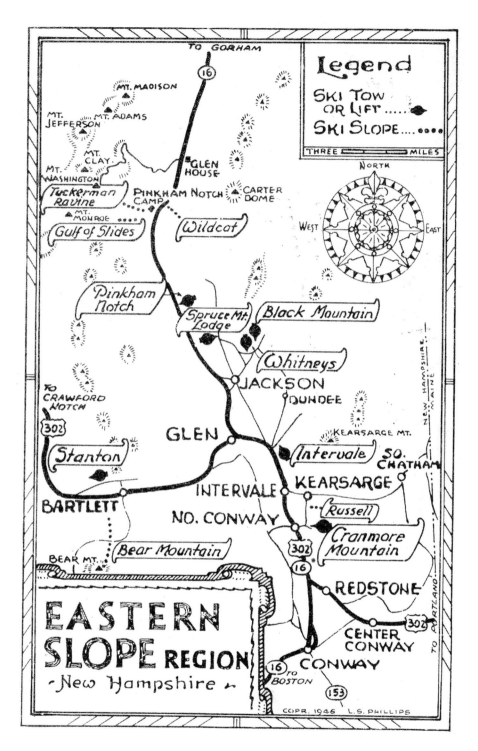

The Eastern Slope Region of New Hampshire includes many lost ski areas. This 1946 postcard shows the locations of the following lost ski areas: Pinkham Notch Omer Giles Tow, Spruce Mountain Lodge, Intervale, Stanton Slopes and Russell's. Whitney's is not lost, but is now the beginner J-bar slope at Black Mountain.

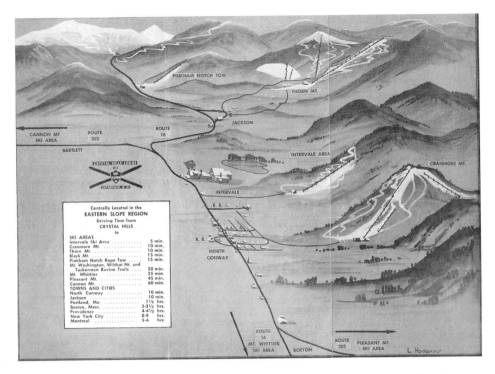

This 1950s map from the Crystal Hills Ski Dorm in Intervale shows some trail maps from lost ski areas. Intervale's open slope and trails are clearly seen. Thorn Mountain's lifts and trails are found above Intervale, but also include unaffiliated Black Mountain, which is not labeled. Pinkham Notch's rope tow and slope can also be seen. *Courtesy New England Ski Museum.*

The Pinkham Notch Ski Lift was operated by Omer Giles. According to Emily Langford, he was an electrician who had seen all of the rope tows that developed in the 1930s around New England and wished to own his own. Bill Currier remembers that the tow was constructed by George Morton, who had built nearby Cranmore's Skimobile. This undated photo shows the construction of the ski area, which took place at some point in the 1940s. *Courtesy New England Ski Museum.*

An aerial view shows the ski area after construction was finished. Note its easy-to-access location just off Route 16. Wide-open slopes with scattered trees provided interest for skiers. *Courtesy New England Ski Museum.*

This February 1950 view of the ski area shows the primary slope, with the rope tow at the far right. The convenient access of the ski area right off Route 16 allowed skiers to access the slope directly from their cars. *Courtesy George Putnam.*

The Schussverein Ski Club held annual ski races at Pinkham Notch along with other clubs. According to Emily Langford, since Omer Giles provided them with electrical work at their ski house in Bartlett, the club naturally held its races at his ski area.

The ski area closed in the late 1950s, likely due to increasing nearby competition, including from the nearby and much larger Wildcat. By March of 2008, the ski slope had grown in, but is still somewhat noticeable. The land was also for sale. *Courtesy Fred Schaaff.*

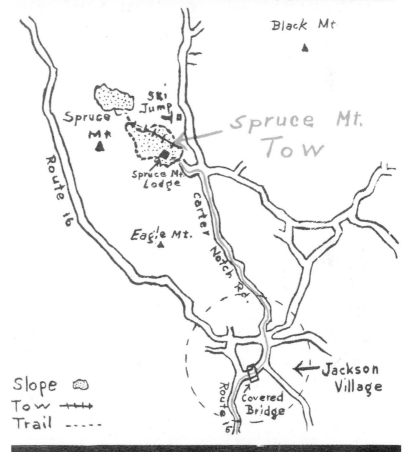

SPRUCE MOUNTAIN SKI TOW

JACKSON, N. H.

ON SPRUCE MOUNTAIN 2 MILES NORTH OF THE FAMOUS SKI VILLAGE OF JACKSON

WE INVITE YOUR PATRONAGE

Spruce Mountain Lodge, originally owned by Mabel E. Slade, opened a nine-hundred-foot-long Underwood rope tow in the mid-1930s in Jackson. The ski area had a wide-open slope that was connected to the longer (three-fourths of a mile) Spruce Mountain Trail above the actual ski area. Slade took good care of her guests, and this 1937 brochure states that the "needs of skiers are given special attention and the Lodge provides an abundance of wholesome, home-cooked foods."

Spruce Mountain Lodge, Jackson, New Hampshire

This early 1950s photograph shows the lodge, with the ski slope in the background. Later, the ownership transferred to the Winquist family and then to Bernie Mallard, who replaced the rope tow with a one-thousand-foot-long Poma lift in 1965. According to Herb Barnes, Mallard worked directly with Jacques Pomagalski, the lift's French inventor. About a dozen cabins and a pool were added to the resort. Mallard then sold the area to Hosni Khalifa, who was from Pakistan and worked for the United Nations. However, the business was not profitable, likely due to competition from much larger resorts nearby, and he put the ski area up for sale.

Herb and Liese Barnes, along with Charlie and Carol Barnes, purchased the area in 1972, in order to open a residential rehabilitation center for disturbed and delinquent kids. Skiing was incorporated into the treatment. According to Stephen Barnes (Herb and Liese's son), while mostly closed to the public, Spruce did open on Monday nights to students from the Jackson Grammar School. The Barneses sold the ski area in 1976 to a jewelry firm from Rhode Island that was going to make Spruce a corporate retreat, but that was not to be. The Poma was sold to Whaleback Ski Area. Today, the resort is posted as private property. This 1950s view shows the ski area in winter, along with the cabins and the lodge.

Thorn Mountain Ski Area in Jackson was built in 1948, and opened for the 1948–49 ski season. Actually located on Middle Mountain, Thorn Mountain was the first ski area in New England to open with two chairlifts, and was one of the largest ski areas in the state of New Hampshire from the late 1940s to the 1950s. This advertisement appeared in the 1948–49 *American Ski Annual* and touted the new ski area.

Charles Plumb (pictured here), also known as C.C. Plumb, was the principal man behind the development, along with C. Bird Keach. Jack MacPherson served as the field superintendent, assisting in the operation of the ski area. Plumb owned a company that produced road-building material and asphalt called C.C. Plumb Co. in Warwick, Rhode Island. Both Plumb and Keach had never seen skiers before they started the development of Thorn, but had heard about the skiing boom taking place and wanted to capitalize on it. *Courtesy Susan May.*

One of Thorn Mountain's drawbacks was this steep access road, shown here after the end of construction in 1948. The road would be quite icy in the winter, with cars often sliding off the road. *Courtesy Sharon Parent, from her father John MacPherson.*

Walter Stadig of Soldier Pond, Maine, manufactured several single chairlifts in New England in the 1940s, including the two at Thorn Mountain. These chairlifts had wooden towers, unlike today's steel towers. The lower chairlift is nearly complete in this 1948 view. The very steep Hogback Slope is just to the right of the chair; it scared away many novice skiers since this was the first slope that was visible. *Courtesy Sharon Parent.*

Porcupine

CHAIR LIFT

GOFF AREA

Bobcat

Plumb Line

OTTER SLOPE

ROPE TOW

Q.B.

PANORAMA

Q.B. | Cub

Vulture's Gulch

Big Birch

Home Run

PLUMMET SLOPE | HOGBACK

COZY CANYON PRACTICE SLOPE

CHAIR LIFT

Zeer's Hill

Cub

ROPE TOW

ROUTE 16-A

JACKSON VILLAGE

JACKSON R.R.

ROUTE 16

JACKSON • NEW HAMPSHIRE

Thorn Mountain had numerous trails and slopes for all levels of skiing. This 1950s trail map shows the two single chairs, along with two rope-tow areas on the Panorama and Cozy Canyon Slopes. One narrow trail was called Plumb Line, a play on owner C.C. Plumb's name. The vast majority of the mountain was not visible from the base. Arthur Doucette of the Jackson Ski School and Hannes Schneider, Skimeister from Cranmore, advised Plumb on the trail construction. *Courtesy New England Ski Museum.*

THORN MOUNTAIN SKI AREA

TRAILS

Q. B. (Quiet Birdmen)	2 mi.	— Novice
Porcupine	1¼ mi.	— Intermediate
Cub	¾ mi.	— Intermediate
Plumb Line	1 mi.	— Expert
Big Birch (Via Bobcat)	1½ mi.	— Expert
Big Birch (Via Otter)	1¼ mi.	— Expert

SLOPES

Panorama	Novice (Tow)
Cozy Canyon	Novice to Intermediate (Tow)
Goff	Novice
Otter	Intermediate (Tow)
Hogback	Expert — 30° Slalom
Zeke's Hill	Expert — 30° Slalom

OTHER FACILITIES

Warming Houses (Halfway, Base, Summit); Restaurants (Halfway, Base); Night skiing every Saturday, or any other night by arrangement. Ski Patrol.

THORN IS EASY TO REACH

BY TRAIN — Daily from Boston, New York, Portland (Intervale Station. Arrange with your hotel in advance for transportation from train).

BY BUS — Interstate Bus Lines.

BY CAR — Route 1 from Boston to Portsmouth; Route 16 to Jackson. Roads plowed and sanded all winter and kept in excellent condition.

Portland	71 mi.
Boston	146 mi.
New York	352 mi.
Philadelphia	440 mi.

Right: Another advertisement in the 1950s lists Thorn's amenities. The base area and Halfway Station both had restaurants, with warming huts featured at the base, middle and summit. The expert Zeke's Hill and Hogback both had thirty-degree slopes. *Courtesy New England Ski Museum.*

Below: This base area postcard by Tom Darville shows skiers boarding the single wooden chairlift. The base lodge/restaurant is at the right end of the parking lot. *Courtesy Susan May.*

Parking was very close to the chairlift, so these skiers did not need to walk very far. The Hogback Slope is on the right, along with the aptly named Plummet Slope on the left side of the chairlift. *Courtesy Sharon Parent.*

The lower chairlift line followed a cut through the ground, as the chairs rode very close to the surface. This view was taken near the top of the lower single chairlift. *Courtesy New England Ski Museum.*

After disembarking from the lower chairlift, skiers could either head back to the base, or continue on to the upper chairlift, pictured here. *Courtesy Sharon Parent.*

A jaw-dropping view of Mount Washington was one of the hallmarks of skiing at Thorn, as this rider on the single chairlift surely enjoyed. *Courtesy Sharon Parent.*

The Halfway Station was a mid-mountain lodge that served up lunches to hungry skiers. In this springtime view, skiers are sprawled out along the deck, and even on the roof, catching some rays. The open-air pavilion on the right was used for summer clambakes. *Courtesy Susan May, taken by H.C. Williams.*

Rhode Island clambakes were popular events at Thorn in the 1950s, held on Saturday afternoons. Tourists would ride the lower chairlift to the Halfway Station to enjoy these clambakes. The menu included "chowder, clams, lobster, fish, sausage, white and sweet potatoes, corn on the cob, lots of butter—for only $3.75." *Courtesy Ken Williams, taken by H.C. Williams.*

This single chairlift was not required to have a safety bar at the time, unlike how it would today. The chairs rode close the ground, though, so any skier that might have accidentally fallen off was not likely to be seriously hurt. *Courtesy Susan May.*

This Tom Darville postcard shows how low the chairs actually rode to the ground. Skiing was not permitted underneath the chairlift, for obvious reasons.

Dick May is shown waxing his skis at the summit warming hut. May was a part of the ski patrol and also repaired skis at the mountain among other jobs. His wife Jonnie worked at the mountain as a secretary to Mr. Plumb, and also sold tickets. Note the chairlift in the background. This hut allowed skiers a chance to warm up before heading down the half-dozen trails from the summit. While the vertical drop was advertised as 1,300 feet, it was actually closer to 1,000. *Courtesy Susan May, taken by Bill Keefe.*

The Q.B. Novice Trail allowed beginner skiers a chance to ski from the top. This easy but narrow trail snaked its way down the mountain. Susan May, the daughter of Dick and Jonnie May, remembers that this trail was quite a workout, as there were several flat stretches. This early Tucker Sno-Cat was used to pack the trail. *Courtesy Sharon Parent, taken by H.C. Williams.*

Left: The Porcupine Trail also descended from the summit. Here, a skier heads down the trail, with Tin Mountain in the background. *Courtesy Susan May.*

Below: An early Tucker Sno-Cat is shown grooming the Panorama Slopes. These slopes were served by a rope tow and provided an excellent view of Mount Washington, in the upper right. *Courtesy Sharon Parent, taken by H.C. Williams.*

Right: The Cozy Canyon Rope Tow was located on a novice/practice slope at the lower right of the ski area. Thorn closed at the end of the 1956–57 ski season. The chairlifts were removed, and portions of the machinery became T-bars at Mount Whittier in West Ossipee. Sold for a price of $2,000, they were the cheapest chairlifts ever sold. Thorn Mountain became the first major ski area to close in New England. *Courtesy Ken Williams, taken by H.C. Williams.*

Below: Forty years later, in 1999, Chris Bradford found the sign for the Cozy Canyon Rope Tow. Bullet-ridden, bent and faded, the sign is still legible. After Thorn closed, parts of this rope tow went to a small ski area in Newport, New Hampshire, according to Bill Currier. *Courtesy Chris Bradford.*

In 2007, the lower liftline for the single chairlift had grown in tremendously, so much that it is almost impossible to find. It can just be made out in the lower left, running diagonally across this image to the upper right. The collapsed engine house is seen in the lower left. *Courtesy Susan May.*

Above: Washington Boulder, also known as Profile Rock, is named for its resemblance to George Washington, though some, including Susan May, liken it more to Alfred Hitchcock. This rock used to lie in the middle of the Goff Area Slope—you can see this profile on the trail map shown on page 72. *Courtesy Susan May.*

Right: Tyrol Ski Area in Jackson opened during the 1962–63 season. Founded by Murray Dearborn, the ski area first opened with a T-bar and several trails on Thorn Mountain. Though it is confusing, Thorn Mountain Ski Area operated on Middle Mountain, and Tyrol Ski Area operated on Thorn Mountain. Dearborn's daughter, Sandra Schmiedeknecht, grew up at Tyrol and also taught skiing there. This ski patch alludes to the famous skiing region of central Europe of the same name. *Courtesy Woodward Bousquet.*

Above: From inside the lodge, guests could overlook the lower slopes and watch skiers board the T-bar. *Courtesy Dick Smith.*

Opposite above: Chalets were built around the base area, and some incorporated spectacular views of Mount Washington. With a view like this, who wouldn't want to purchase one? *Courtesy Dick Smith.*

Opposite below: The ski lodge faced due south, which allowed skiers to enjoy the sunshine. The lodge also housed a Jack Frost Ski Shop and a cafeteria. In addition to the ski area, owners could also enjoy a clubhouse with a bar and a swimming pool. *Courtesy Dick Smith.*

The original T-bar lift rose from just outside the lodge to the summit, with a parallel Poma lift on the left that went one-third of the way to the top. Jackson Falls, a steep and uncrowded mogul run, is shown to the right of the liftline. Just beyond Jackson Falls and not pictured here was Frostee—a trail so steep that snowcats could not groom it. The trail often featured icy moguls and thin cover. *Courtesy Dick Smith.*

The Poma lift, built in 1965, allowed beginners and intermediate-level skiers to enjoy the wide slope on the right. This slope was also used each spring near Easter for the annual "Silly Slalom," when kids would don costumes and ski from one obstacle to the next. This was a favorite activity for younger skiers in the 1960s. Many other races and events made Tyrol the leader in activities in the Mount Washington Valley. *Courtesy Sandra Schmiedeknecht.*

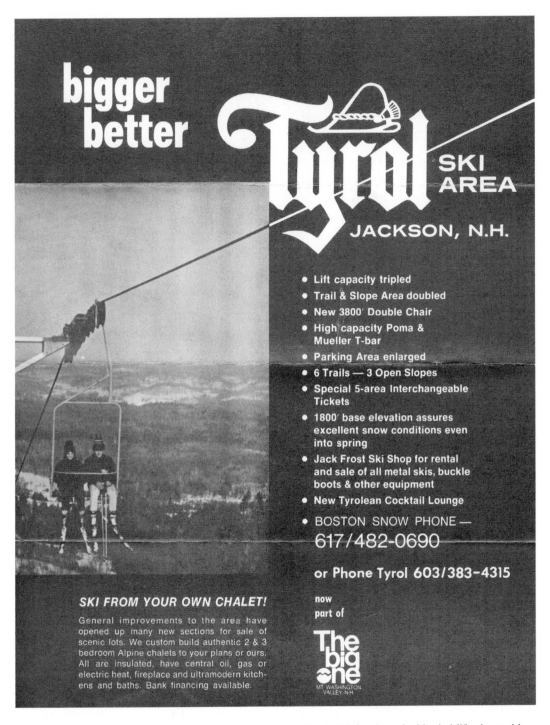

In 1968, Tyrol dramatically expanded the ski area by adding this 3,800-foot-long double chairlift, along with additional trails and slopes. This allowed the ski area to be in the same league with nearby larger ski areas such as Black Mountain, Attitash, Wildcat and Cranmore. An interchangeable ticket with all of those areas was offered to boost skier visits. *Courtesy New England Ski Museum.*

Calvin Dearborn, the youngest son of owner Murray Dearborn, rides up the chairlift with Suzie, the family's St. Bernard dog, during the inaugural 1968–69 season. The one-thousand-foot vertical chairlift began below the lodge to the east. This did pose a problem if a skier became injured on the slopes below the lodge. Bob Maguire remembers that the ski patrol would have to load the skier into a toboggan, ski down to the chairlift, load the skier onto the lift, unload at the top and ski down to the ski patrol headquarters. *Courtesy Sandra Schmiedeknecht.*

Just like the single chairlift at nearby Thorn Mountain, skiers were treated to impressive views of Mount Washington on the ride up the double chairlift. *Courtesy Dick Smith.*

Left: A wide-open slope near the summit fed into Upper and Lower Doubleheader, the slope underneath the chairlift. Taken from the chairlift, this view of the slope shows a scattering of trees, which allowed for more interesting skiing. *Courtesy Dick Smith.*

Below: Ski patrol also enjoyed a wide-open view of Mount Washington from their hut on the mountain. Pictured here are Duck Schofield (left) and Freddie Guptil (right). *Courtesy Sandra Schmiedeknecht.*

Murray Dearborn sold Tyrol in the early 1970s to Tim and Peter Bailey, who continued to operate the ski area until about 1980. Strong competition, a steep access road and a lack of snow making led to Tyrol's demise. Most of the trails have grown in, as seen in this late 1990s aerial view, though some are still recognizable. The long swath on the left was the chairlift, and you can also see some of the chalets on the lower portions of the slopes. The land and lodge that was Tyrol is now on private property. *Courtesy NASA World Wind.*

IRON MOUNTAIN HOUSE

WHERE YOU GET "MORE FOR LESS"

IRON MOUNTAIN HOUSE offers a friendly and informal atmosphere at reasonable rates.

Our excellent home cooked food is served cafeteria style, eliminating waitresses and tipping. The top three floors are our sleeping quarters which feature double bunks during the winter months and a choice of beds or bunks during the summer months. Most rooms have sinks with adjoining baths.

We have a dance hall which is ideal for large gatherings. The Knotty Pine Rumpus room is great for smaller gatherings. Four fireplaces provide a pleasant background for cozy wintertime get togethers.

IN THE EASTERN SLOPE REGION

Our own ski slope and tow equipped with lights for night skiing

Above left: Jack and Evelyn Butler owned the Iron Mountain House in Jackson from the 1960s to the 1990s, and operated a small rope-tow ski area for guests. This 1960s brochure shows the Iron Mountain House. Nearby larger ski areas Black Mountain, Wildcat and Cranmore were advertised.

Above right: There was only one slope served by an eight-hundred-foot rope tow. In a story told by Dick May to Tom Eastman, this rope tow was the same tow that had operated at Thorn Mountain, Cranmore, Stanton Slopes and the May Brothers Tow! According to Evelyn Butler, high school students from Berlin helped run the lift. Nighttime skiing was available, and in fact was one of the few such areas where it was possible. The lower image here from the brochure shows the slope on the lower portions of Duck Head.

The ski area closed in the mid-1970s. According to Jack Butler, significant competition and higher minimum wage rates made his small ski area unaffordable to operate. Sadly, on August 30, 2000, the Iron Mountain House suffered a major fire. This February 2002 view shows the fire damage. The building was soon torn down, and now the Red Fox Grille operates on the premises.

The ski slope adjacent to the Red Fox Grille has not been developed. The former wide-open slope has grown in tremendously, but is still faintly visible below Duck Head. *Courtesy Fred Schaaff.*

It is hard to believe that skiers once enjoyed this wide-open slope at Iron Mountain, as tree growth has been rapid. Most of the rope tow towers still stand, though the trees are now five to ten times taller! *Courtesy Dan Robertson.*

Stanton Slopes in Bartlett was owned and operated by Woodbury and Lizzie Stanton from the late 1930s to the early 1940s. The Civilian Conservation Corps helped clear the land for the future ski area during the late 1930s. This postcard view shows the wide-open slope, including the ticket booth at the base. *Courtesy Art Donahue.*

Many farms opened rope tows in New England in the 1930s in order to attract a little winter business, and Stanton was no exception. According to Dick May, the rope tow originally was installed at the lower slopes of Thorn Mountain in 1936–37, then was moved to Cranmore a year later and then finally to Stanton Slopes. This promotional 1941 calendar shows that the Stantons also operated a dairy farm. *Courtesy Dale Trecarten.*

This late 1930s view shows skiers looking out across the slope. One famous ski area founder, Peter Seibert, lived with his family in a rented second farmhouse on the property in the late 1930s. Seibert would go on to serve in the Tenth Mountain Division, and he later founded Vail in Colorado. Woody Stanton passed away in January of 1941, and his family continued the ski area operation through the rest of the winter before closing. *Courtesy Dale Trecarten.*

However, Stanton Slopes would reopen in 1953 as the local chamber of commerce leased the ski area from the Stanton family. The ski area would operate for five or six more years before closing for good. The slopes grew in substantially, and the nearby land was sold and is now a housing development called Stillings Grant. This 2002 photo shows the ticket house that the Stantons had moved years earlier closer to the farmhouse for easier use. *Courtesy Art Donahue.*

The top engine house still stands as of 2006. The original engine was mounted to the four concrete pillars inside the building. The ski area land is protected as common land within the Stillings Grant development and should remain undeveloped. *Courtesy Fred Schaaff.*

Intervale Ski Area, in Intervale, was a long-lasting ski area that operated from the mid-1930s to the mid-1970s. It was part of Fred Pabst's Ski Tows Inc. chain of ski areas that operated in New England and the Midwest from the late 1930s to the early 1940s. A "hook-type tow," otherwise known as a J-bar, served a wide-open slope and trail in its initial years. In the mid-1940s, the ski area was sold to Dick Stimpson, pictured here. *Courtesy Rich Stimpson.*

Dick Stimpson originally worked at the New England Inn and used to bring guests to Intervale to teach them to ski. Stimpson also ran a successful tennis court construction business in Hyannisport, Massachusetts, where he also worked as tennis instructor in the summer. *Courtesy Rich Stimpson.*

Intervale featured this cozy base lodge, encased here in icicles. A snack bar operated inside the lodge, and according to Tim Greene sold "milk for three cents, and hot dogs for a nickel" in the late 1950s and early 1960s. Greene also remembers that the lifts would shut down for thirty minutes during lunch, which was a practice at some ski areas at that time. *Courtesy Rich Stimpson.*

Access to the ski area was a bit of a challenge. Skiers would park on Town Hall Road and would have to cross this narrow footbridge over the East Branch of the Saco River to arrive at the ski area. The sign above the lift lightheartedly reminds crossers to "Watch Their Bridgework." *Courtesy George Putnam.*

This thirty-meter jump was the location of many competitions during the 1950s and 1960s. Located on the right-hand side of the slope, the jump was often used by nearby high schools' skiing programs. *Courtesy Rich Stimpson.*

Right: Racing was a popular event at many smaller ski areas. While smaller ski areas like Intervale could not compare to nearby larger ski areas in terms of vertical drop and number of trails, events like racing and jumping kept the excitement level high. Here, Emily Langford negotiates a racecourse during the 1955 annual Schussverein-Drifters Husband and Wives Ski Club Race. *Courtesy Emily Langford.*

Below: The original J-bar lift was removed upon the sale of Intervale to Dick and Priscilla Stimpson. The lift was reinstalled at Bromley Mountain in Vermont and was replaced by this 1,500-foot-long rope. Originally installed on the right side of the slope, it was moved to this location on the left in the early 1950s. *Courtesy Rich Stimpson, taken by Peter Besh.*

Above: This 1950s trail map shows all the facilities and trails at Intervale. Besides the wide-open slope, a narrow "Twister" trail from the top allowed skiers a winding way back to the base. A much longer novice "Maple Villa," named after the Maple Villa Inn in Intervale, was also available.

Opposite above: A Poma lift replaced the long rope tow in 1956, allowing for a much more comfortable ride. Construction equipment is shown here clearing and grading the liftline. *Courtesy Rich Stimpson.*

Opposite below: Once installed, the Poma lift proved quite popular, as this liftline proves. While lines occasionally built up, they were always shorter than those for the Skimobile at nearby Mount Cranmore. The Poma lift would be removed in 1986, about ten years after Intervale closed. The lift was purchased by Landry's Ski Slope in Windham, New Hampshire, but was never installed. Mr. Landry also sold parts of the lift to the Atlantic Forest Ski Area in Amesbury, Massachusetts. *Courtesy Dick Smith.*

In the early 1970s, Intervale was leased out to Eastern Mountain Sports, which used the area for Nordic skiing, but this ultimately failed. Strong competition and the inability to expand the land above the ski area led to the closing of the ski area. The slope grew in rapidly, and in 2008 is hardly noticeable. The land and lodge remain in the Stimpson family. This 1950s view shows the wide-open view from the summit. *Courtesy Rich Stimpson.*

Russells, located in Kearsarge, billed itself as having "complete facilities for all winter sports." Located just three-fourths of a mile from Mount Cranmore, Russells was well suited to capitalize on the rapid growth of skiing in North Conway. While they offered their own ski slope, they clearly used the background of Mount Cranmore in this brochure as a promotion.

Russells had more facilities in the 1940s than many resorts do today. Along with a lighted ski slope, they offered a lighted toboggan chute, recreation hall, lighted skating ring, several cottages for lodging, dancing and movies.

In the 1930s and 1940s, the ski slope was not lift served, as shown in this postcard. Skiers would have to earn their turns. Tobogganers also used the ski slope in tandem with skiers.

In the early 1940s, a temporary rope tow was set up for one weekend at Russells. John Nutter and Nathan Nichols had built a ski tow for use elsewhere in Massachusetts, but had promised to bring it to Russells for a certain weekend. As there was no snow in Massachusetts, this 1932 Ford, nicknamed "Oswald," was driven to Russells and briefly converted into a rope tow. *Courtesy John Nutter, provided by Sandy Nichols Ward, daughter of Nathan Nichols.*

Before Oswald's brief stint as a ski lift, it was the family car for Nathan and Janet Nichols, given to them by Nathan's great-aunt May in 1940. May had tried to sell the car to a dealer, but he only offered eighteen dollars—she knew it was worth more, and gave it to the Nicholses as a wedding gift. Many years later, after its brief use at Russells, Sandy Nichols Ward learned how to drive using this car—what a history! *Courtesy John Nutter.*

The soon-to-be Mrs. John Nutter, also known as "Bunny," is shown here skiing down the slope at Russells during this special weekend. While Oswald would shortly return to Massachusetts, a permanent nine-hundred-foot-long tow was erected at Russells in the late 1940s and operated into the 1950s. *Courtesy John Nutter.*

Lost Ski Areas of the Conway, Tamworth and West Ossipee Region

This region was the eastern gateway to the White Mountains. Route 16 allowed many skiers quick access to ski areas farther north. Locations in this region tried to capture some of that traffic. Mount Whittier in West Ossipee is a prime example. Located at the junction of Routes 16 and 25, this mountain couldn't be missed by skiers heading to North Conway. Its facilities, including a gondola and summer attractions, were very much on par with more northern ski areas. However, poor snowfalls, a lack of snow making and a lack of intermediate and easier terrain led to its demise.

Most other ski areas in this region were served by small rope tows, often at hotels or inns, and occasionally in farmers' fields. The Tamworth Outing Club was a big promoter of skiing in the region, and was involved with Page Hill, Ferncroft and Quimby Hill.

Additional lost ski areas not pictured include:

Bald Hill Lodge, Conway: Located on Route 16, the lodge ran a 1,500-foot tow on an intermediate slope during weekends, holidays and by appointment.

Beck's Lodge, Conway: This lodge operated a 600-foot-long rope tow, with slopes available for night skiing. Used mainly by guests in the early 1950s, the area was open weekends and holidays, and also by appointment.

Oak Hill Twin Trails, Conway: Located one and a half miles south of Conway on Oak Hill, this small ski area had a 675-foot-long rope tow. The area operated from the late 1930s to the early 1940s. It was described in a guidebook as having "plenty of space for beginners, but chiefly of interest to the expert."

Jackson Farm Tow, Conway: First known as the Jackson Farm Tow in the late 1930s, this area became the Hillside Farm tow in 1940. Owned by Arthur Jackson, he would allow some skiers to pack down the slopes manually for free tickets, according to Arthur King. The area had closed by 1950.

Freedom Tow, Freedom: Freedom Ski Tow operated during the 1940s, offering an intermediate "schuss" that was accessed from a 1,000-foot rope tow.

Ferncroft Inn, Wonalancet: A 500-foot-long rope tow served a 100-foot-wide slope behind the Ferncroft Inn in the early 1940s.

Dundee Mountain Lodge in Conway, New Hampshire, operated a small T-bar ski area from the late 1960s to the mid-1970s. According to Paul Getchell, Richard Cutliffe acquired several tracts of land in South Conway on Dundee Mountain in 1965. He soon lost financing, but in the late 1960s, with the help of twenty-six friends and relatives, Mr. Cutliffe created the Dundee Mount Corporation and got the project back on track. An 1,800-foot-long T-bar was constructed and served a single, north-facing slope, along with a rough trail from the summit. *Courtesy Paul Getchell.*

DEEP SNOW COUNTRY

ALWAYS PLENTY OF SNOW

PANORAMIC VIEW

DESIGNED FOR THE NOVICE
INTERMEDIATE

For Groups of 40 or more.....DUNDEE
LODGE is yours for the WEEK END.
Get your RESERVATION in now for the
WEEK END OF YOUR CHOICE.

No equipment necessary....OUR OWN
SKI RENTAL SHOP.

FREE RENTAL of Ice Skates.

900 PER HOUR LIFT CAPACITY MEANS
MORE SKI TIME...NO WAITING.

FOR THE EXPERT SKIERS.............
SEVEN MAJOR MOUNTAINS JUST
MINUTES AWAY.
        EXCELLENT CUISINE
        ALL YOU CAN EAT

DANCE AND FUN

SIT 'N' SIP

Above: The Dundee Mountain Lodge offered a dormitory and enticed large groups of students and skiers mainly from the Boston area. Other recreational activities were also offered. Competition against already-established ski areas and the oil shocks of the mid-1970s took their toll at Dundee, and the area was foreclosed in 1976. The T-bar was sold to Oh-Ho-Ho Ski Area in Connecticut for $4,000, and several homes were developed high up on the slopes. *Courtesy Paul Getchell.*

Right: John and Libby Edge owned and operated the Rockhouse Mountain Farm tow from the 1950s to the 1970s. The farm was a complete winter and summer resort, with many outdoor activities, including skiing, tobogganing, farm activities, archery, badminton and much more. Three rope tows, including the one shown here across the street from the farm, allowed guests to ski in a family atmosphere. *Courtesy Johnny Edge.*

Rockhouse Mountain Farm
A SMALL COUNTRY INN
EATON CENTER, NEW HAMPSHIRE

FOR YOUR
Family Vacation
IN WINTER

The primary rope tow was located across the Rockhouse Mountain Farm in a hayfield that overlooked the low mountains of western Maine. The line denotes the location of the rope tow. A few additional trails and a rope tow were also briefly located in the hill behind the farm. *Courtesy Johnny Edge.*

This postcard view shows that while the tow was quite short, four hundred feet long, a short practice racecourse could still be used. In fact, the Edges' children, Johnny and Betsy, would practice here with the Kennett High School Ski Team. Sadly, winter operations ceased in 1976, and the farm itself closed in 2006. *Courtesy E. John Allen.*

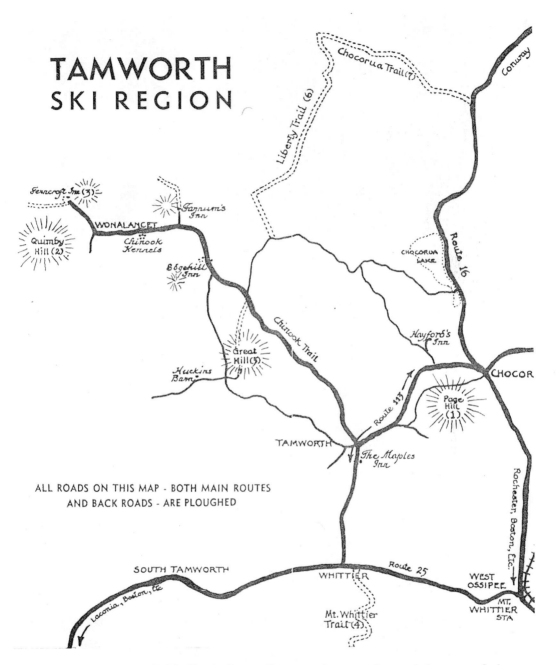

TAMWORTH
SKI REGION

ALL ROADS ON THIS MAP - BOTH MAIN ROUTES
AND BACK ROADS - ARE PLOUGHED

The Tamworth Ski Region billed itself as having excellent snow closer to major population centers farther south. In this 1940s map, several lost ski areas, including Page Hill, Ferncroft Inn and Quimby Hill, are labeled. Other non-lift-served trails are shown as well, including the original Mount Whittier Ski Trail. *Courtesy Cook Memorial Library Archives.*

Left: Tamworth Outing Club operated a ski area on Page Hill in Tamworth from the 1940s. An eight-hundred-foot-long tow served the steep five-acre ski area. Al Campagna remembers that the snack bar at Page Hill was self-serve—and skiers would pay using the honor system. Here, a skier heads downhill on the steep slope. *Courtesy Cook Memorial Library Archives.*

Below: As larger resorts in the North Conway region developed, skiing faded away at Page Hill, and was over by the 1960s. While much of the slope is now forest, a small portion remains clear, with excellent views of Whiteface Mountain in the background. *Courtesy Jeremy Clark.*

Above: A small rope tow operated in Quimby Hill in Wonalancet during the 1940s and 1950s. This rustic shelter was used not only in the winter at the ski area, but also in the summer for campers and hikers. *Courtesy Cook Memorial Library Archives.*

Right: The Mittlebirge Slopes, located at the junction of Routes 16 and 25 in West Ossipee, opened in the early 1950s. It boasted this early Platterpull lift, which was built on a wide-open and fairly steep slope. In 1957, the area would be sold and renamed Mount Whittier. Mount Whittier greatly expanded in the late 1950s, adding more slopes and T-bars, the latter built from salvaged materials from the single chairlifts at Thorn Mountain. *Courtesy Dick Smith.*

Above: Mount Whittier, at the gateway to the White Mountains, was a highly visible and substantial ski area in the 1960s. In the mid-1960s, Mount Whittier had a gondola, three T-bars and three rope tows. While there were slopes and trails for all classes of skiers, complex double fall lines and icy conditions made a lot of the skiing quite difficult. Trails were named after the works of poet John Greenleaf Whittier.

Left: In 1963, a four-passenger Mueller gondola, the first four-passenger ski lift in New England, was built at Mount Whittier. At nearly one and a quarter miles long, with a vertical of 1,300 feet, the gondola was also one of the most significant lifts in New Hampshire at that time. This scene shows the gondola shortly after construction was finalized, on a day when the lift was being tested. *Courtesy Dick Smith.*

Lost Ski Areas of the Conway, Tamworth and West Ossipee Region

Right: In order to ride the gondola, skiers would board the lift across Route 16, ride over the road and enter a midstation shortly thereafter. At this point, they could disembark and choose to access a nearby T-bar or continue to the summit. Riders had this impressive view of Ossipee Lake to the east. *Courtesy Dick Smith.*

Below: The gondola was used not only by skiers, but by summer sightseers as well. For only one dollar and fifty cents, tourists could start their journey at this gondola base station, where snacks and souvenirs were also sold. Upon arriving at the summit, they were treated to views of Mount Washington, the Presidential Range, the Sandwich Range, the Ossipees, Ossipee and Silver Lake, Mount Chocorua and even Portland Harbor!

Left: The original A-frame lodge was quite small in this late 1950s photos. While the ski slopes faced northeast, these skiers are angled southwest, enjoying the sunshine. *Courtesy Dick Smith.*

Below: In the mid-1960s, the base lodge expanded, with even a larger base lodge coming later in Whittier's existence. The easily accessible location proved a hit with skiers, as this jammed parking lot suggests. The Whittier Slope T-bar is visible on the wide-open slope behind the lodge. This lift replaced the original Platterpull about 1960.

While many of the trails at Whittier were challenging, beginners could learn on the twin rope tows of Fanny Hill. The Harry Baxter Ski School taught many to ski at Mount Whittier. Above Fanny Hill is the Bear Camp Slope (left) and the Whittier Slope (right). *Courtesy Dick Smith.*

This early 1980s trail map shows that little had changed from twenty years earlier in terms of lifts and slopes. Various summer activities, including a monorail mountain slide and summer skiing on roller skis, were not enough to keep Whittier in business, and the area closed in 1985. Whittier was briefly resurrected as Mount Madness, an outdoor adventure center, in the late 1990s and early 2000s, but organized skiing was not offered. A handle tow was installed on the Hobbs Slope and briefly served a snow-tubing operation, but that did not last, and the tow has now made its way to a private ski area in upstate New York.

The next several photos give a good idea of how the passage of time can wreak havoc on a lost ski area. At the top of Mount Whittier, skiers could enjoy this summit cafeteria that was located in the gondola building. The summit lodge was also used in the summer, shown here as tourists enjoy its deck in the 1960s.

Forty years later, this 2008 view paints a very different picture. Vandalism and harsh New England weather have taken their toll on the gondola unload building and summit lodge. Windows have been smashed, the deck is in serious disrepair and tree growth has begun around the building. *Courtesy Jeremy Clark.*

Tourists and skiers alike had an excellent view from the summit of Mount Whittier. Looking down the liftline at the top gave excellent views of Silver Lake and Madison to the east from this fall view in the 1960s.

A 2008 view illustrates that, from this angle, not much has changed. The same towers shown in the previous photo still stand, as does the power pole to the right. Silver Lake is clearly visible. *Courtesy Jeremy Clark.*

One of the more interesting views to be found at a lost ski area is this juxtaposition of modern life and ski history. Taken in March of 2007, this lower gondola tower still stands and has hardly changed since it was built in 1963. Meanwhile, a McDonald's been built in the parking lot of the former gondola base, and a Subway is now located across Route 16.

The gondola midstation is still standing in 2007, but is slowly disappearing in the undergrowth. The former liftline for the gondola has also seen a significant amount of tree growth, but each and every tower remains as it was forty years ago.

The Survivors

Today, only a few "classic" rope tow ski areas still operate in the White Mountains. While sixty areas have closed, these survivors have managed to beat the odds, and provide a living glimpse into what skiing was like decades ago. These ski areas allow families to ski at a cost much more affordable than at a larger resort.

There is a strong need for these small ski areas to remain open. They provide a healthy and fun form of exercise, which can be a factor in the fight against childhood obesity. They form strong community bonds between the operators, volunteers and skiers. And they also allow people to look forward to winter instead of dreading it.

There are only two rope tow ski areas still in existence in the White Mountains. Mount Prospect, which is located just south of Lancaster on Route 3, had been closed since the late 1990s, but was able to reopen in 2008. This ski area has had a long past, and now looks forward to a bright future. A borrowed Yurt now serves as a base lodge, the Thiokol "Sprite" groomer has been refurbished, trails have been cleared and the classic sign now hangs proudly on Route 3.

Kancamagus Ski Area, located on the Kancamagus Recreation Road in Lincoln, is a thriving small ski area. While used mostly by younger skiers, adults enjoy the slope as well. Ski teams practice here and are able to make many laps on the fast rope tow. Years ago, Loon Mountain donated snow making equipment, so that the "Kanc" could open even in lean years. Skiers would often learn to ski at smaller ski areas and then progress to the larger resorts, and this continues from the "Kanc" to Loon.

With the possibility of high energy costs in the future reducing long-distance ski vacations for some, families may once again turn to smaller community ski areas for recreation. This may even reopen a few of the closed ones. Strong and consistent community support is a must for these smaller ski areas that are often run by volunteers.

If you wish to experience what skiing was like decades ago, when life and skiing were simpler, then be sure to visit the Kancamagus and Mount Prospect Ski Areas.

Mount Prospect Ski Tow in Lancaster is a long-duration ski area that has recently reopened. The Lancaster Outing Club originally maintained a novice trail on Mount Prospect called the Sinclair Weeks Trail in the 1930s. In the 1940s, the Outing Club would open this one-thousand-foot-long rope tow on Mount Prospect. The lift served three slopes. *Courtesy Warren Bartlett.*

One of the ski slopes in the 1960s at Mount Prospect is pictured here. The base lodge can also be seen, which featured a small snack bar. Generations of families learned to ski here until the mid-1990s, when Mount Prospect closed. The lodge roof unfortunately collapsed in 1999, but the slopes were still kept relatively clear during this period. *Courtesy Warren Bartlett.*

Plans to reopen the ski area began in the mid-2000s, and in 2005 the people of Lancaster overwhelmingly voted to support a substantial bequest to the club to cover the high cost of insurance. The rope tow was refurbished, as was the groomer, and a borrowed Yurt was set up to be used as a base lodge. The area briefly operated in 2008 but is now well positioned for the future, allowing the next generation of skiers to enjoy this historic treasure. This early 2008 view shows the several ski slopes of Mount Prospect, located one and a half miles south of Lancaster on Route 3. *Courtesy Neil Brodein.*

The Kancamagus Recreation Area in Lincoln began full operation in 1946, though it was originally referred to as the Lincoln Ski Tow. Quent Boyle remembers that in April of 1946 a motor from the nearby mill was brought over to the ski area and was converted into a rope tow that served the left side of this slope. Edmond Gionet was the first operator of the lift. In the 1950s, the tow was lengthened and moved to the right-hand side. This 2008 view shows the rope tow on the right, serving the wide-open slopes on the left.

Today, the Kancamagus Recreation Area is operated by the Lincoln-Woodstock Recreation Department, and allows residents and guests to ski at an extremely affordable price. Nighttime skiing is available. For more information, please visit the Recreation Department's Website at http://www.lincolnnh.org.

Conclusions

Sadly, the loss of sixty ski areas in the White Mountains Region has had a negative impact, though some impacts are hard to measure. It has become somewhat more difficult for less affluent people to learn how to ski, or to take their families on a weeklong vacation that they could have enjoyed at one of these small ski areas.

Many of the lost ski areas were quite small, with just a rope tow and a few slopes. But almost all of them allowed families to ski for very low rates, and all allowed for a cozier atmosphere not commonly found today at larger ski areas.

Of course, larger ski areas offer a completely different product than many of the lost areas did. It is hard to fathom what ski-area founders in the 1930s and 1940s would have thought of today's high-speed quads, manicured grooming, massive snowmaking coverage and slopeside hotels. Today's larger areas provide for a much more varied ski experience that smaller ski areas certainly could not provide.

Preserving the ski history of all these lost areas is very important and must be continued. As time moves steadily forward, many of the early ski pioneers pass away. Their rich experiences and knowledge are lost. Photographs and brochures of these lost ski areas may become tossed aside, lost forever.

If you enjoy ski history, there is much you can do to help save it. First, by joining the New England Ski Museum, you can become a member of an organization dedicated to saving the ski history of New Hampshire and New England. The museum hosts annual events, including an Apres Ski Party, the annual banquet featuring the Spirit of Skiing Award, the Exhibit Opening Party, the annual Hannes Schneider Memorial Meister Cup Race and much more. It also allows you to connect to the larger community of ski history enthusiasts. Located in Franconia Notch at the base of the Cannon Mountain Tramway, the museum is easy to reach. For more information on the museum, please visit http://www.skimuseum.org, or call 603.823.7177.

Additionally, the New England Lost Ski Areas Project (NELSAP) is a huge online resource on all of the lost ski areas mentioned in this book. If you liked the histories presented here, you can learn even more by visiting http://www.nelsap.org. Each lost ski area has its own page, with photos, personal memories, trail maps and much more.

Conclusions

It is time to save the history of these now lost places. Perhaps you know someone who was involved with one of these defunct ski areas. Maybe you skied or worked at one of them. You might have even come across a stash of old postcards and brochures in your attic. You are invited to share your knowledge with NELSAP, preserving it online forever. Please visit the website for more details on how you can be a part of saving the history of lost ski areas.

Finally, you can help prevent still-operating areas from closing simply by patronizing them. From the surviving rope tow areas to other small ski areas, your support can mean the difference between becoming lost and staying open.

About the Author

Jeremy Davis grew up in Chelmsford, Massachusetts, learning to ski at nearby Nashoba Valley. While a teenager, Jeremy frequently explored lost ski areas throughout New England. Boy Scouting helped grow his love of the outdoors, and he earned the Eagle Scout award. In 1998, while a student at Lyndon State College in Lyndonville Vermont, Jeremy founded the New England Lost Ski Areas Project. In 2000, Jeremy was elected to the New England Ski Museum Board of Directors, where he continues as a Board member. He is a senior meteorologist with a private weather forecasting company, and resides near Saratoga Springs, New York.

Visit us at
www.historypress.net